IMAGES
of America

THE GREAT SMOKY
MOUNTAINS
NATIONAL PARK

IMAGES
of America

THE GREAT SMOKY MOUNTAINS NATIONAL PARK

Steve Cotham

ARCADIA
PUBLISHING

Published by Arcadia Publishing
Charleston SC, Chicago IL, Portsmouth NH, San Francisco CA

Printed in the United States of America

Library of Congress Catalog Card Number: 2006929835

For all general information contact Arcadia Publishing at:
Telephone 843-853-2070
Fax 843-853-0044
E-mail sales@arcadiapublishing.com
For customer service and orders:
Toll-Free 1-888-313-2665

Visit us on the Internet at www.arcadiapublishing.com

CONTENTS

ACKNOWLEDGMENTS

This book was a personal labor of love, but it was not the work of one person. I am grateful to Larry Frank, director of the Knox County Public Library System, for encouraging this project and to the staff of the Calvin M. McClung Historical Collection for their help and support.

But I must especially thank Sally R. Polhemus, archivist of the Calvin M. McClung Historical Collection, for her help with many aspects of putting together this book. Her knowledge of the major photograph collections in the library was invaluable as was her knowledge of photographs included in various manuscript collections. Her help and advice in searching through hundreds of potential photographs was key to any success that the published work may accrue. Other staff also assisted in the search for photographs. I am grateful for the special efforts of Helen Bryant, Diana Hall, and Brenda Hampton. And last but not least, I must thank Laura Martin, my assistant, for typing almost all of the text of this book from nearly illegible handwriting.

I would also like to thank Annette Hartigan, archivist of the Great Smoky Mountains National Park Archives, for her assistance with photographs in park archives. Her professionalism and courtesy were much appreciated.

All proceeds from the sale of this book will accrue to the benefit of the Calvin M. McClung Historical Collection, from which the majority of the photographs in this volume were drawn. Any errors in the book are to be laid to my charge, not to any of those who assisted me.

—Steve Cotham

INTRODUCTION

In the half century that has elapsed since the 1950s, where the story told in this book ends, the Great Smoky Mountains National Park has faced enormous challenges. Then the infrastructure of the park was just being completed, after having been slowed by World War II. Gatlinburg was becoming a very successful small resort town, although strictly seasonal. Pigeon Forge was still rich farmland, with just a few tourist-oriented establishments springing up. In the 21st century, the amazing growth of the area outside the park has literally changed the landscape.

Today the Great Smoky Mountains National Park faces a number of specific challenges. It is the most visited of all the national parks in the United States, with over nine million visitors per year, twice as many as second-place Grand Canyon National Park. Air pollution has become a very serious problem. What was once the landmark haze of clouds and fog hanging around the peaks of the Great Smoky Mountains is now likely to be smog from automobile exhaust and coal-fired power plants. Air pollution has dramatically affected some plant and animal life. New insect pests, accidentally imported from abroad, threaten new devastation in the park. Most notable are the adelgids, which threaten to destroy the Fraser firs and hemlocks, great stands of which are a major feature of the landscape of the park.

On the plus side, the biological diversity of the Great Smoky Mountains National Park has been documented more thoroughly than ever before. The Friends of the Great Smoky Mountains National Park and the Great Smoky Mountains Association provide advocacy and financial assistance to the park, which has been significantly underfunded and is legally prohibited from charging any form of admission by the terms of the original agreement creating the park.

Perhaps the single biggest threat to the future of the Great Smoky Mountains National Park is massive development, which is taking place on the fringes of the park, especially on the Tennessee side. The endless proliferation of vacation chalets and retirement homes around the edges of park is becoming a problem. When bears occasionally wander out of park boundaries seeking food, they stumble onto these enclaves of housing, where they—not the new residents on the doorstep of the park—are seen as the problem. As development continues to grow denser along the Tennessee border of the park, this situation will only get worse. It is a great shame that the Great Smoky Mountains National Park did not reach the original boundaries first proposed for it, which would have reached out as far as Chilhowee Mountain. But at least we have the half-million acres protected within the park, for which every citizen of this country should be most grateful. This haven of biodiversity will adapt and survive to delight visitors for many years to come.

One of the most famous scenic spots in the Great Smoky Mountains is this view of Alum Cave Bluff on Mount LeConte. The hikers in this photograph, which was taken in the 1920s, are dwarfed by the immense overhang of rock face above them. (Thompson Collection, Calvin M. McClung Historical Collection.)

One

EARLY SETTLEMENT OF THE GREAT SMOKY MOUNTAINS

Archaeologists tell us that people have inhabited the Great Smoky Mountains for perhaps as long as 12,000 years. Different Native American cultures came and went over the millennia. Hernando de Soto visited what is now East Tennessee in 1539 in his fruitless search for gold and riches among the Native American peoples of what is now the southeastern United States. Significant contact with the Overhill Cherokees of East Tennessee began in the early 1700s when the colony of South Carolina inaugurated a lucrative trade in deer hides with the Cherokees. At the height of the commerce in deer hides, over 50,000 hides per year were traded to merchants in Charleston for sale at home in the colonies or in Great Britain.

In the decade after the end of the French and Indian War (1754–1763), European settlers began to migrate into the Great Valley of East Tennessee, despite strong prohibitions from the British government. Several decades of intermittent warfare between the settlers and the Cherokees were followed at last by peace and by the inevitable transfer of title to lands in Tennessee from the Cherokees to the government. A series of treaties over 50 years gradually extinguished Cherokee claims to all but a relatively small portion of southeast Tennessee.

Settlement of the Great Valley of East Tennessee took place first, but settlers began to move into the coves and valleys of the Great Smoky Mountains, particularly in the period from 1810 to 1840. Herds of livestock from as far away as Knoxville were brought to the balds, grassy meadows high on the summits of the mountains, for summer pasture, especially in the years before the Civil War. Before the railroad arrived, livestock were driven to market on foot, traveling the roads to market from one "stand," a simple inn with pens for the animals, to the next.

Sentiment during the Civil War was divided between Union and Confederate, although sentiment for the Union predominated in the six mountain counties that are now part of the Great Smoky Mountains National Park. Many of the Cherokees from Qualla across the Great Smoky Mountains, however, joined the Confederate army.

Tourism can be said to have begun with the hotels built near mountain mineral springs, such as Montvale, Line Springs, and Henderson Springs. In the late 19th century, commercial logging began in the Great Smoky Mountains on a large scale.

This steel engraving of the Great Smoky Mountains in North Carolina was published in 1872 in the book *Picturesque America*. The view of the highest mountains in the eastern United States, wreathed in a timeless mist, was one of the first images of these mountains to be made widely available to the public. (Calvin M. McClung Historical Collection.)

Drury Paine Armstrong (1799–1856) of Knoxville was one of the largest individual landowners in the Great Smoky Mountains in the antebellum era. At one time, he held title to over 50,000 acres of mountain land, almost 10 percent of the present acreage of the park. Mountain tenant farmers operated a large farm called Glen Alpine on part of this land. His grandfather Col. Samuel Wear (1750–1817) was a Revolutionary War soldier and a pioneer settler of Wears Cove, near modern-day Pigeon Forge, arriving perhaps as early as 1780. (Calvin M. McClung Historical Collection.)

Herds of sheep and cattle were pastured in summers on the grassy balds in the high elevations of the Great Smoky Mountains. Many of these herds came from farms miles away in the valley. This photograph, taken in 1907 by S. H. Essary, shows a flock of sheep on Spence Field. (Harvey Broome, Calvin M. McClung Historical Collection.)

This rare early photograph of a herder cabin was taken in 1890. The photograph was probably taken near one of the balds around Cades Cove in the Great Smoky Mountains. (W. O. Garner, Blount County Public Library.)

Herds of animals, even flocks of turkeys and geese, were driven to the market on foot in the antebellum era. The animals were walked from one "stand" to the next. The "stand" was a tavern with pens for the animals to stay overnight. This engraving, from *Harper's New Monthly Magazine* in 1857, shows a herd of pigs being driven to market from the mountains of East Tennessee. (Calvin M. McClung Historical Collection.)

William G. Brownlow (1805–1877), the fiery Methodist minister, Unionist, and newspaper editor from Knoxville, hid out in Tuckaleechee Cove among friendly Unionists when Confederate authorities sought his arrest on charges of treason in 1861. Brownlow returned to Knoxville with the victorious Union army in 1863 and took up his vitriolic pen as editor of his newly renamed newspaper, the *Knoxville Whig and Rebel Ventilator*. (Calvin M. McClung Historical Collection.)

Mountain farmers marked their hogs and let them run free to forage for nuts and other mast in the hills and mountains. The wild boar, however, is a big-game animal that was imported by hunters into Western North Carolina in 1912. It escaped into the wild in the Great Smoky Mountains and is very destructive of plant life and habitat. This photograph shows a herd of swine at Spence Field near Thunderhead in July 1915. S. H. Essary is at left in the photograph. (Harvey Broome, Calvin M. McClung Historical Collection.)

This panoramic view shows Cherokee, North Carolina, around 1904. The "Oconolufti" River (so spelled on the back of the photograph) flows through the town. Travel in the mountains by horseback or in a horse-drawn vehicle was slow and difficult, not to be undertaken by the faint-hearted. (Calvin M. McClung Historical Collection.)

Charles Christopher Krutch (1849–1934) was a Knoxville photographer and musician. He was also an amateur painter in oil and watercolor whose great passion was to paint landscapes of the Great Smoky Mountains. Each summer he would spend up to six weeks boarding with mountain families and hiking and sketching mountain scenes. He would return home and paint mountain landscapes in his studio from sketches and from memory. Toward the end of his life, he became widely known regionally as a painter, dubbed the "Corot of the South" after French landscape painter Jean-Baptiste-Camille Corot. (Thompson Collection, Calvin M. McClung Historical Collection.)

Two

THE CHEROKEES OF QUALLA

By the dawn of the 17th century, the Cherokee people had established a claim over a vast territory in parts of present-day North and South Carolina, Georgia, Tennessee, and Kentucky. The principal Cherokee settlements were on both the eastern and western sides of the Great Smoky Mountains and along the upper reaches of the Savannah River.

A very prosperous trade in deerskins with merchants in Virginia and South Carolina began in 1673 and persisted through the next century. The Cherokee Nation disastrously chose to back the French over the English in the French and Indian War (1754–1763) and then the British over the Americans in the American Revolution (1775–1783). As settlers poured into modern-day Tennessee and Kentucky after 1769, the Cherokees fought a fierce intermittent war with the new settlers through the end of the century.

Although the Cherokees readily adopted the agricultural lifestyle of the new settlers after 1790, they were gradually "persuaded" to cede most of the ancestral land they had previously claimed. The Treaty of New Echota (1835) required the Cherokees to cede the rest of their homeland and to move west to the Indian Territory, now Oklahoma. During the forced removal of the Cherokees in 1838 by the U.S. Army, it is estimated that one quarter of 16,000 Cherokee people died in route.

A small number of the Cherokees who lived at what is now the Cherokee Indian Reservation at Qualla successfully resisted removal in 1838. A number of fugitives from among the Cherokees rounded up for forced removal managed to join the band at Qualla. The legendary figure Tsali, who had supposedly killed a U.S. soldier, surrendered and was executed with his sons so that his people might be left undisturbed in North Carolina.

Between 1875 and 1880, the U.S. government officially recognized the Eastern Band of the Cherokees and the boundaries of their reservation. From 1887 to 1890, Smithsonian anthropologist James Mooney did fieldwork with the Cherokees at Qualla and recorded their history, myths, sacred rites, and tribal culture. The Cherokee Fair, held annually in October since 1914, created a market for the sale of tribal handicrafts and encouraged the preservation of traditional culture. The creation of the Great Smoky Mountains National Park in 1934 made the Cherokees dependent on tourism as a major source of income. The town of Cherokee was, and is, the major eastern entrance to the park.

The town of Cherokee was also known as Yellow Hill, or "El-la-wa-dah." This photograph originally belonged to Miss Lucy Luttrell, matron of the Cherokee Indian School in 1905. (Calvin M. McClung Historical Collection.)

This photograph, taken in 1903 at the Reunion of Confederate Veterans in New Orleans, shows the group of surviving Cherokee soldiers of Thomas's Legion. This is the last known photograph taken of this group of soldiers. Will Thomas, their former leader, died in 1893. (Great Smoky Mountains National Park Archives.)

This photograph shows the neat and prosperous-looking log house of Tom Tally, located on Stillwell Branch in the Cherokee Indian Reservation in 1939. (H. C. Wilbur, Great Smoky Mountains National Park Archives.)

Nancy George Bradley weaves a basket in front of her home on Wrights Creek around 1930. (Great Smoky Mountains National Park Archives.)

Members of the Robert Bigmeat family make traditional Cherokee clay pots and figurines in front of their home on Wrights Creek in 1940. Examples of their craftsmanship are on the table where they are working. (H. C. Wilbur, Great Smoky Mountains National Park Archives.)

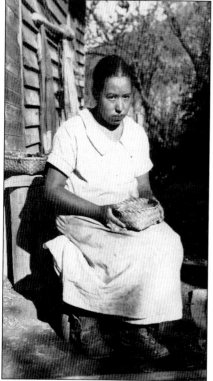

Oevlie Tooni Du-na'-e, the stepdaughter of Chief Standing Deer, is shown seated holding a double-weave basket she had made in 1936. The art of double-weave basketry was almost lost before the revival of this ancient craft in the 1930s. (C. S. Grossman, Great Smoky Mountains National Park Archives.)

Irene Swimmer stands in front of a display
of traditional Cherokee crafts for sale at
the Cherokee Indian Fair on October 7,
1932. (Harvey Broome, Calvin M. McClung
Historical Collection.)

A Cherokee woman is intent on weaving a
basket as a small boy quietly watches her work at
the Cherokee Indian Fair around 1930. (Carlos
Campbell, Great Smoky Mountains National
Park Archives.)

Cherokee men compete in an archery contest at the Cherokee Indian Fair in 1932. (Great Smoky Mountains National Park Archives.)

The score is tallied for the competitors in an archery contest at the fair. (Harvey Broome, Calvin M. McClung Historical Collection.)

A man demonstrates the use of a blowgun at the Cherokee Indian Fair on October 7, 1932. Notice how he holds the gun near his mouth, not farther out. As the small wooden arrow with a thick tuft of thistle is launched with a puff of air, he steadies the gun so that it can accurately hit a target 30 yards away. (Harvey Broome, Calvin M. McClung Historical Collection.)

Cherokee women perform the traditional Green Corn Dance at the Cherokee Indian Fair in March 1926. (Great Smoky Mountains National Park Archives.)

The traditional Cherokee game of "stick ball" was played for tourists as part of the Cherokee Indian Fair on October 7, 1932. The players are scrambling for the ball, which can only be lifted from the ground with the player's rackets. Stick ball is a very rough-and-tumble game, with elements similar to lacrosse, soccer, football, wrestling, and boxing. Here the players are shown in action on the field. (Harvey Broome, Calvin M. McClung Historical Collection.)

The man in a hat in the foreground holding the long switch is the "captain" of one team of stick-ball players. He sometimes uses the long stick to spur on slow players. He can also pick up and return to players ball sticks dropped during the game. Most players played ball barefoot, wearing only a pair of short trunks. (Harvey Broome, Calvin M. McClung Historical Collection.)

Oevlie Tooni Du-na'-e, the stepdaughter of Chief Standing Deer, demonstrates the traditional method of grinding corn with a mortar and pestle at the Cherokee Indian Fair on October 8, 1935. (H. M. Jennison, Great Smoky Mountains National Park Archives.)

Andrew Otter (left), Irene Swimmer (center), and Runaway Swimmer attend the Cherokee Indian Fair on October 7, 1932. The Swimmers lived in Sweeney, North Carolina. (Great Smoky Mountains National Park Archives.)

Jarrett Blythe, chief of the Cherokee Indian Reservation, attends the Cherokee Indian Fair on October 7, 1932. Chief Blythe was only 41 when he was elected to a four-year term as chief. He did not speak the Cherokee language and predicted it would be dead in a few generations. The council, composed of Chief Jarrett Blythe, Vice Chief Andrew Otter, and Agent Salisbury, administered the affairs of the reservation. (Great Smoky Mountains National Park Archives.)

In June 1937, the Cherokee Indian Fair was taken on the road to Knoxville to see if it would be a successful fund-raiser across the mountains in Tennessee. Events were staged at Caswell Park. A Cherokee delegation, who just received the key to the City of Knoxville, gave a headdress to a city father. (Thompson Collection, Calvin M. McClung Historical Collection.)

Three

LOGGING IN THE GREAT SMOKY MOUNTAINS

The massive stands of timber and the many varieties of trees in the Great Smoky Mountains were recognized as a great source of potential wealth decades before commercial logging became feasible. Early logging in the Great Smoky Mountains was local in scope, designed to fill the needs of nearby communities. Since waterpower was readily available for operating water-powered saws and since logs were plentiful, frame buildings replaced many of the earlier log structures.

Tanning leather became a profitable enterprise because abundant chestnut, hemlock, and oak bark from logging provided key ingredients for processing leather. Schlosser Leather Company operated a substantial tannery in Walland from 1902 to 1931, during the logging boom.

The pace of logging in the Great Smoky Mountains picked up dramatically after 1900, as the railroad became part of commercial timber-cutting operations. Speculators for large northern lumber companies with substantial capital began to buy up valuable stands of timber. The Little River Lumber Company, started by Col. Wilson B. Townsend of Pennsylvania, was established in 1900. It chartered the Little River Railroad in 1901 and built an extension of the Southern Railroad up the Little River Valley. By 1908, logging operations had moved up the Little River as far as Elkmont.

At the height of the logging boom, over 200 miles of railroad snaked through the mountains. Geared locomotives, such as the Shay engine, pulled heavy loads through the steep and winding terrain. Portable steam-powered machines, such as the Clyde Overhead Skidder and the Surrey Parker, made loading and moving large logs by rail much easier and safer. Large lumber mills and company towns were built at Crestmont on Big Creek; Smokemont on the Oconoluftee River; Ravensford on Raven Fork; Townsend on the Little River; and Proctor on Hazel Creek, among others. The logging itself was done from portable camps, which moved from site to site as needed. The books *Dorie* by Florence Cope Bush and *Last Train to Elkmont* by Vic Weals movingly document what life was like in the lumber camps of the Little River. Logging continued on much of the land acquired for the park. In 1939, the Little River Lumber Company hauled its last load of logs from the mountains to its mill in Townsend. Over 60 percent of the Great Smoky Mountains National Park had been logged by 1940, when the park was dedicated.

This photograph shows the Swaggerty and Eubanks Lumber Company in the 1880s in Elkmont. This was the first serious, although local, logging done there. This lumber company built the first wagon road to connect Elkmont and Sevierville by way of Blanket Mountain, Metcalf Bottom, and Wears Valley. (Great Smoky Mountains National Park Archives.)

George Washington Shults and some neighbors snake a large log down the mountain using a team of six oxen. (Great Smoky Mountains National Park Archives.)

A group of lumbermen rest after cutting a large tree in Elkmont. This photograph was taken around 1910. (Calvin M. McClung Historical Collection.)

A steam shovel is used to build the roadbed and lay track up the Little River Gorge for the Little River Railroad around 1906. (Great Smoky Mountains National Park Archives.)

In 1925, this enormous hollow chestnut tree grew in the Middle Prong of the Little River, above Tremont. Jim Shelton, the photographer, posed his family around—and inside—the tree. Shelton later cut the tree, rolled it down the bank, and used it as a wall to retain fill dirt for the railroad bed. Mrs. Shelton (Caroline Walker) standing at the left of the tree was one of the famous Walker sisters of the Greenbrier. The Shelton children, from left to right, are John (inside the tree), Geena, Effie, and Hazel. (Jim Shelton, Great Smoky Mountains National Park Archives.)

Sam Cook's cabin, above Elkmont, partly obscures the view of the portable houses of the logging community in the distance. Sam Cook served as a mountain guide to hunters and hikers in the Smokies in the 1920s and 1930s. (Laura Thornburgh, Great Smoky Mountains National Park Archives.)

The steam-powered Surrey (pronounced "Sary" by the loggers) Parker log-loader is shown here loading a heavy log onto a railroad "flat-car" above Elkmont around 1918. (Great Smoky Mountains National Park Archives.)

These contract loggers are working for the Little River Lumber Company on Blanket Mountain around 1922. Their work tools are the "S" hook, held by Jim Shelton, who's resting on the log, and the "grabs," visible behind the legs of the horses. Ashly Perman is driving the team. (Great Smoky Mountains National Park Archives.)

A log is shown traveling down the "skid road," which was built through Mids Branch above Elkmont to bring logs off the mountain around 1910. (Great Smoky Mountains National Park Archives.)

Four men are seen here peeling tan bark from large trees, probably hemlocks. Tan bark found a ready local market at the Schlosser Leather Company at Walland, which operated from 1902 to 1931. (Great Smoky Mountains National Park Archives.)

The "swinging railroad bridge," as it looked in 1918, was built below Meigs Falls near the mouth of Meigs Creek. The bridge was suspended in air between the rock bluff and the wooden trestles at the right of the photograph. The children on the level track to the left of the photograph may be the family of the photographer. (Jim Shelton, Great Smoky Mountains National Park Archives.)

This photograph shows the logging camp at Forks Fish Camp and Rough Creek. The temporary housing is set very near the railroad among the logs and "slash," the limbs and other waste parts of the felled trees. The building with the windows set at a diamond-shaped angle is the commissary. (Great Smoky Mountains National Park Archives.)

The operations of the new Little River Lumber Company were the subject of a feature article in the *Hardwood Record* in 1909. Photographs celebrated the variety of large hardwood trees and the size of some of the large specimens that were cut. (Calvin M. McClung Historical Collection.)

Little River Lumber Company Townsend Mill No. 2 stands behind the log pond, where logs were held until they were milled into lumber. This mill was built in 1916 and rebuilt after it burned on June 23 of that year. It continued to operate until July 5, 1939. (Great Smoky Mountains National Park Archives.)

The Little River Railroad Engine 110 stands in the rail yard in Townsend in the 1920s. This engine pulled the funeral train of any employee of the Little River Lumber Company who died and took the mourners to the funeral. The train also carried the body of Margaret Townsend, first wife of Col. W. B. Townsend, from the funeral at the family home in Townsend to Knoxville for burial in Old Gray Cemetery on January 7, 1924. (Great Smoky Mountains National Park Archives.)

The Little River Lumber Company camp store at Fish Camp, above Elkmont, is seen here, perched precariously between two converging lines of railroad track around 1915. (Great Smoky Mountains National Park Archives.)

Joe Murphy Sr., superintendent of Little River Railroad, sits at the wheel of the Model T Ford inspection car used by the railroad around 1908. The car had been fitted with flanged wheels to run on the railroad track. The car could make quick, economical trips between the mill at Townsend and Elkmont. In 1911, the automobile was destroyed when it unexpectedly met up with locomotive No. 110 on the track. (Great Smoky Mountains National Park Archives.)

The Little River Railroad Motor Car No. 1 provided quick and easy travel for a larger number of people between Townsend and Elkmont after the Ford motorcar was destroyed in 1911. One person described it as "that wonderful bus at Elkmont." (Great Smoky Mountains National Park Archives.)

This building served as both the local church and school in Tremont around 1920. Moving pictures were also sometimes shown in this building at night, with electricity for the movie projector provided from a generator run by the river current nearby. Locals referred to this building, jokingly, as the "house of salvation, education, and damnation." (Great Smoky Mountains National Park Archives.)

This aerial view shows the Crestmont Lumber Company lumber mill at Big Creek in North Carolina, probably in the 1920s. Beyond the millpond at the left of the photograph are the mill buildings, railroad cars on the tracks, and piles of boards in the background. (Great Smoky Mountains National Park Archives.)

This photograph shows the temporary logging camp (Camp 18) at Three Forks Prong, probably in the 1920s. The portable houses were transported on railroad cars, offloaded, and then linked together in a row, commonly called a "string town" by the workers. The mountainside around the camp is mostly clear-cut and stripped of trees. (Great Smoky Mountains National Park Archives.)

Logging in some parts of the newly designated park continued up until near the official dedication in 1940. This photograph, taken July 5, 1939, shows three officials of the Little River Lumber Company—Marvin Tipton (left), "Doc" Tipton (center), and Joe Murphy Jr. (right)—standing next to the last log to go through the lumber mill at Townsend. (Great Smoky Mountains National Park Archives.)

Four

THE PEOPLE OF THE MOUNTAINS

The people of the Great Smoky Mountains were dogged by stereotypes almost from the time that they first arrived in the mountains. They were often referred to as "mountain whites," which suggested a kinship and connection to the "poor whites" of the Deep South. While the economic status is not entirely inaccurate, the important fact is that the mountain people were not driven into the mountains by poverty but chose to live their lives there.

The popular image of the violent, ignorant mountain moonshiner came from writers of "local color" fiction, who promoted the idea that the mountaineers were a "peculiar people" living in a "strange land." While there were some prosperous farmers in the larger coves, many mountain families did lead hard and simple lives. One thing that all the mountain people shared was a degree of isolation caused by bad roads, often virtually impassable for any kind of vehicle. Trade was limited, but travel on horseback and on foot was much less restricted. Mountain communities were physically isolated, but community churches and schools, often combined in one building, were centers of social life.

A quite different and romantic image of the mountaineers became popular in some quarters in the 20th century. Mountain people were seen as a "lost tribe" of the early pioneer settlers of North America, who had preserved a pure remnant of pioneer American life. This romantic image was nurtured by the idea that the mountain people spoke a "pure Elizabethan" dialect of English, a concept promoted by some early students of dialect, ballads, and folklore.

The term "hillbilly," a 20th-century invention, first appeared in print in 1900 in an article about poor whites living in the hills of northern Alabama. By the 1920s, hillbilly was used more generally to describe the mountain whites of Appalachia. The term was imbued with ridicule and condescension—much like the words "cracker" and "redneck." Some mountain people have embraced the term hillbilly and rewritten the definition of the word in a positive light to set their culture apart from the mainstream. Some tourist attractions in the mountain resorts have exploited the hillbilly stereotype to make money, just as some of the Cherokees at Qualla have adopted Native American dress from the tribes of the Great Plains to cater to tourists whose knowledge of Native American culture is derived solely from movies and television.

This photograph from the 1920s shows what photographer Jim Thompson described in his caption as "a typical mountaineer's cabin." Thompson took two versions of this photograph, one with and one without people. (Thompson Collection, Calvin M. McClung Historical Collection.)

Mary Noailles Murphree (1850–1922) is shown in this portrait as a young woman. She wrote under the pen name Charles Egbert Craddock. In 14 novels and in over 40 short stories, she drew heavily on memories and impressions of mountain life and people made during visits to Beersheba Spring in the Cumberland Mountains and to the Great Smoky Mountains in the 1870s and 1880s. She presented mountain people as quaint, peculiar, backward, and largely unassimilated to American society. Her somewhat negative view of mountain people and mountain life colored public perception for decades. Though acclaimed in her lifetime, she is largely unread today. (Calvin M. McClung Historical Collection.)

This photograph shows a mountain family traveling on foot at Indian Gap around 1911. The mule is heavily laden with sacks. (Harvey Broome, Calvin M. McClung Historical Collection.)

A small boy travels by horseback at Roaring Fork near Gatlinburg around 1930. (Harvey Broome, Calvin M. McClung Historical Collection.)

Around 1906, a young hunter stands proudly with his hog rifle and powder horn. Despite the large chestnut stump behind him, heavy logging was just beginning. Hunting was still good in these years. As logging continued, game became scarcer. (Great Smoky Mountains National Park Archives.)

SAM BURCHFIELD, VETERAN MOONSHINER OF THE APPALACHIANS

This postcard shows Sam Burchfield, labeled here as a "veteran moonshiner of the Appalachians." Burchfield of Chestnut Flats was selected to be "the" representative mountaineer at the Appalachian Exposition held in Knoxville in 1910. (Great Smoky Mountains National Park Archives.)

W. O. Garner took this early photograph of a "wildcat still" in Cades Cove around 1890. (W. O. Garner, Blount County Public Library.)

This rare 1890s photograph shows the interior of a Cades Cove still with the barrels and buckets used in storing and processing moonshine. (W. O. Garner, Blount County Public Library.)

Two men with a hunting dog display their bear traps. The population of black bears declined drastically during the period of heavy logging in the first half of the 20th century. (Great Smoky Mountains National Park Archives.)

In this photograph taken in November 1926, I. T. McCarter is seen holding both a fiddle and a rifle. Presumably these were two of his most prized possessions. (Laura Thornburgh, Great Smoky Mountains National Park Archives.)

Clementine Enloe of Ravensford, North Carolina, goes fishing around 1936. Joseph Hall, the photographer, was told that if he took her a box of a snuff as a present, she would let him take her picture. The box of snuff can be seen in this photograph tucked in her blouse. (Great Smoky Mountains National Park Archives.)

Manning McCarter is seen here hiking Mount LeConte at age 86. He had hiked the mountain many times during his life. His first hike was as a young man during the Civil War. (Thompson Collection, Calvin M. McClung Historical Collection.)

Celia Profitt Ownby, widow of John Ownby, cards cotton. The cotton "batts," sheets of combed cotton, were used inside quilts for insulation and to give the quilts thickness. (C. S. Grossman, Great Smoky Mountains National Park Archives.)

Mrs. Will Saunoosking demonstrates the art of spinning on her high wheel on the porch of her house in the Cherokee Indian Reservation in 1940. (H. C. Wilburn, Great Smoky Mountains National Park Archives.)

The family of "the roaming man of the mountains," Wiley Oakley, a mountain guide famous with hikers and hunters, is shown in this photograph on the porch of their cabin near Gatlinburg around 1925. His sculpture, titled *Minnehaha*, sits in front of the family. Oakley is supposed to have said, "I have one woman I talk to, and one who talks to me." (Great Smoky Mountains National Park Archives.)

Rebecca (Mrs. Wiley) Oakley is weaving in this photograph made on June 31, 1937. The settlement school Pi Beta Phi sparked the revival of many mountain crafts such as weaving, especially in the vicinity of Gatlinburg. (Alan Rinehart, Great Smoky Mountains National Park Archives.)

Sofie and Tom Campbell lived on a
mountain near Gatlinburg with only a
foot trail to their cabin. Both of them
lived to be quite old. They are shown
in this photograph with two of their
grandchildren on the porch of their
cabin on November 10, 1931. Note the
steep, cultivated patch of ground behind
the house and the bee gums (hives).
When Sofie died, Civilian Conservation
Corps workers carried her coffin down
the mountain for burial. (George Grant,
Great Smoky Mountains National
Park Archives.)

Sofie Campbell, shown in this pensive
photograph, is sitting outside her cabin
smoking her pipe around 1930. (George
Grant, Great Smoky Mountains
National Park Archives.)

Giles (in the hat) and Lenard Owenby, sons of Jackson Owenby, are seen here sitting on a load of wood shakes rived (split with a froe) by their father on June 21, 1937. (Alan Rinehart, Great Smoky Mountains National Park Archives.)

In this photograph, taken in 1925, a mountain man examines the leaves on a tree and looks curiously at the sign posted on the tree, which reads, "Fire Destroys Forests. Be Careful." (Laura Thornburgh, Great Smoky Mountains National Park Archives.)

Quill (Eagle) Rose holds a scythe to cut hay or wheat. On the porch table behind him are a saddle and bridle. Rose was a well-known storyteller, fiddle player, hunter, and moonshiner. He became friends with Horace Kephart, who lived across the ridge from Eagle Creek. Rose died in 1906 and is buried in a small cemetery in Calderwood. (Great Smoky Mountains National Park Archives.)

Charles and Flora Messer Morrow are shown in this photograph as a young couple. They were married in Cataloochee on November 5, 1916. Her father hired a Knoxville caterer for the wedding, which was easily one of the biggest social events ever held in Cataloochee. Her husband offered her $1000 or land as a wedding gift when they were married. She took the cash. (Great Smoky Mountains National Park Archives.)

Martha June McCarter is hoeing a dry, rocky field of corn, a typical patch of mountain hillside around 1930. (Harry Wolfe, Great Smoky Mountains National Park Archives.)

Wiley Gibson is shown in this photograph, taken around 1930, holding the barrel of a gun on which he is working. Wiley was a member of the third generation of Gibsons who had made guns in the Great Smoky Mountains. (Exline, Great Smoky Mountains National Park Archives.)

This group of musicians from Henderson Springs posed for a group photograph around 1910. The musicians, from left to right, are as follows: (first row) Ollie Carr, Jim Carnes, and Lee Carnes; (second row) Dicie Henderson, Frank Carnes, and Ida Carr. (Sherry Marshall and Agnes Hatcher Marshall.)

In this photograph, taken around 1930, James Grant (Jim) Proffitt is shown playing the guitar and singing for his admiring niece, Grace Newman, on the front porch of the Ples A. Proffitt home (now demolished). (Burton Walcott, Great Smoky Mountains National Park Archives.)

Five

EARLY TOURISM IN THE MOUNTAINS

Tourism in the Great Smoky Mountains can be said to have begun with the hotels built as mineral springs resorts. Montvale Springs, Henderson Springs, Line Springs, Mount Nebo, and Alleghany Springs—to name only a few—were some of the mineral springs hotels around the Great Smoky Mountains that offered spring water, widely believed to be beneficial to the health of those who drank it. Saratoga, New York, was the archetypal American example of an elegant mineral springs resort.

Montvale Springs, once called the "Saratoga of the South," was the leading antebellum mineral springs resort in East Tennessee. Beginning in the 1830s and lasting for just over a century, Montvale was an inn and spa. The first hotel was a large log structure, replaced in 1853 with a much larger and more elegant frame building of three stories with seven gables, surrounded by porches on all three floors. An extensive lawn of 10 to 20 well-landscaped acres formed the grounds. In the summer season, there were typically 300 to 400 boarders. Guests came primarily from Georgia, Alabama, and Louisiana. A brass band played every night for dancing. Arnold Guyot, the Swiss geologist, was a guest at Montvale in 1859, during his trip to map the Great Smoky Mountains and calculate the heights of the peaks. Mount Guyot is named in his honor.

Over the years, there were probably over 20 mineral spring hotels scattered around the lower elevations of the Great Smoky Mountains. These spas flourished, especially from the 1870s to the early 1900s. As the fashion for these holiday resorts waned, most of the buildings were lost either to fire or demolition.

A group of elaborately dressed tourists from Knoxville is ready for what appears to be a fishing trip in 1893. The party was "roughing it" at Linville Gorge in the mountains of Western North Carolina. A series of tents functioned as a dining room, a sitting room, and sleeping quarters. Every luxury of home, including servants, was included with the accommodations. The party in the photograph included, from left to right, F. H. McClung Jr., Anita Reis, Mrs. George Reis, Miss McCrary, and guide Potter Brown. (Calvin M. McClung Historical Collection.)

Guests at Alleghany Springs Hotel are posed on the steps of the hotel in this photograph, taken in 1892. Built in 1886, the hotel was a luxurious resort that featured three types of health-giving spring water from Yellow Springs and Chilhowee Medical Springs, both located nearby. The three-story hotel, which had 60 rooms, was lavishly furnished and equipped with expensive china, crystal, and silver. The hotel was lit by gaslights and offered hot and cold mineral-water baths. Croquet, bowling, tennis, dancing, fishing, boating, and riding were amusements for the guests. The ballroom in the basement could hold 100 dancers. As the fashion for visits to mineral springs waned, the hotel closed in 1915. The building was destroyed by fire December 6, 1932. (Will Parham, Calvin M. McClung Historical Collection.)

A group of guests at the DuPont Springs Hotel poses in front of the hotel around 1912. Knoxville photographer Jim Thompson is included in the group (first row, second from the right). DuPont Springs offered mineral waters and a welcome escape from the heat in the lowlands. The hotel sat high on the crest of Chilhowee, or Bluff, Mountain, facing north toward Knoxville. The Devil's Den and the Buzzard's Wash were popular rock outcrops on the bluff, where guests enjoyed the view of the valley and the distant Cumberland Mountains. (Courtesy of Sally R. Polhemus.)

A group of mountain men help barbecue meat for a picnic meal for visiting tourists around 1915. (Harvey Broome, Calvin M. McClung Historical Collection.)

Ruben T. Cates (1867–1902), a Knoxville lawyer, frequently visited Montvale Springs throughout his life. Every morning he stayed at Montvale, he blew the foxhunting horn on Montvale's Look Rock to awaken the guests. (Calvin M. McClung Historical Collection.)

This photograph shows the Montvale Springs Hotel as it looked in the 1920s, not long before it burned. In the heyday of mineral springs, the hotel was known as the "Saratoga of the South." Sterling Lanier took over management of the hotel in 1857. His son, the poet Sidney Lanier, made Montvale the setting of his novel *Tiger Lilies* (1867). After the Civil War ended, the hotel entered a slow and gradual decline but continued to operate until the mineral springs era ended. The last hotel building on the site burned November 21, 1933. Today the property is a YMCA camp for boys. (Thompson Collection, Calvin M. McClung Historical Collection.)

In this photograph, a young Harvey Broome and his family are enjoying the Knoxville First Methodist Sunday school outing and picnic at Sunshine around 1910. (Harvey Broome, Calvin M. McClung Historical Collection.)

Members of the Elks Club of Knoxville are taking a tour of the Great Smoky Mountains by rail on the Little River Railroad in 1915. Here the group posed for a photograph on a railroad trestle. (Great Smoky Mountains National Park Archives.)

.The mineral springs at Montvale Springs Hotel were always one of its star attractions. Here a hotel employee serves mineral water to guests in 1931. (Thompson Collection, Calvin M. McClung Historical Collection.)

By about 1915, the "Elkmont Special" took tourists from Knoxville through Sunshine to Elkmont daily. The entire trip from Knoxville to Elkmont took at least two and a half hours. In this photograph, the train appears to have stopped for a moment in the Little River Gorge to allow tourists to stretch their legs by the river. (Great Smoky Mountains National Park Archives.)

A young Harvey Broome (1902–1968), future member of the Smoky Mountains Hiking Club and future founder of the Wilderness Society, is seen in this photograph on his first camping trip in the Great Smoky Mountains around 1912. (Harvey Broome, Calvin M. McClung Historical Collection.)

Mary U. Rothrock (1890–1976) was a Knoxville librarian, historian, and writer. She began her long association with Gatlinburg and the Great Smoky Mountains in 1921. Rothrock purchased a cabin in Gatlinburg and entertained many guests there over the years. This photograph from her album shows the road to Rocky Spur on Mount LeConte around 1922. (Mary U. Rothrock, Calvin M. McClung Historical Collection.)

The age of travel by automobile led undeniably to a need for overnight accommodation. Brye made this early version of a foldout camper bed for Hudson and Essex Automobiles in the 1920s. (Thompson Collection, Calvin M. McClung Historical Collection.)

Brye made a slightly plainer version of a tent attachment for resting or overnight sleeping for the Ford automobile in the 1920s. In this photograph, the tent is assembled and ready for use. (Thompson Collection, Calvin M. McClung Historical Collection.)

The employees of Knoxville florists and their families enjoy a picnic at Kinzel Springs and Sunshine in 1915. The entire group is standing around the train engine at the depot at Sunshine. The man with the beard at the far left of the photograph is E. J. Kinzel. (Thompson Collection, Calvin M. McClung Historical Collection.)

This aerial view shows the Little River at Kinzel Springs and Sunshine around 1922. In 1892, E. J. Kinzel bought a tract of land at the western entrance to Tuckaleechee Cove. In 1907, he donated to the International Sunshine Society a tract of land on the north side of the river, where a vacation hotel was built for girls who worked in factories and other jobs in the city. The community became known as Sunshine. In 1914, he built the 28-room Kinzel Springs Hotel, which also had 10 cottages. The hotel operated until 1945. (Thompson Collection, Calvin M. McClung Historical Collection.)

There were a number of "swinging bridges" suspended over the rivers flowing out of the Great Smoky Mountains in the early 20th century. The bridge in this photograph is the one over the Little River at Kinzel Springs as it looked in the 1920s. The sign over the bridge says, "5–10 fine for running or jumping." (Thompson Collection, Calvin M. McClung Historical Collection.)

The front of the hotel at Kinzel Springs is seen here as it looked when it was still new, around 1915. (Thompson Collection, Calvin M. McClung Historical Collection.)

The crowd of happy swimmers is enjoying the cold mountain water in the Little River at Sunshine around 1920. The swimming hole was, and is, one of the more popular and accessible places to swim in the Great Smoky Mountains. (Thompson Collection, Calvin M. McClung Historical Collection.)

The more adventurous mountain tourists could venture up to the Indian Gap Hotel, above Sugarlands, in the 1920s. The rustic hotel, shown in this photograph around 1925, provided easy access to the higher elevations of the Great Smoky Mountains. The hotel was removed from the park in 1933. (Great Smoky Mountains National Park Archives.)

A party of Great Smoky Mountains tourists is shown traveling by horse and mule along one of the trails in the mountains in the 1930s near Gatlinburg. (R. Hanlon, Calvin M. McClung Historical Collection.)

The barely improved road at Roaring Fork near Gatlinburg, seen here as it was in 1922, was one of the better mountain roads in the Great Smoky Mountains before improvements were made to roads for the park. (Mary U. Rothrock, Calvin M. McClung Historical Collection.)

Six

ELKMONT, THE APPALACHIAN CLUB, AND WONDERLAND PARK

Ironically, both logging and tourism came to the Great Smoky Mountains on the same train, the Little River Railroad. After 1901, excursions on the Little River Railroad were popular with Knoxville social clubs. Hunting and fishing were the chief amusements of the founders of the Appalachian Club, but logging soon depleted fish and game. In 1908, Col. Wilson B. Townsend deeded 50 acres on Jakes Creek for a clubhouse and hotel for the Appalachian Club and for lots for individual cabins, which were constructed through the 1920s in areas that came to be known as Society Hill and Daisy Town. Millionaire's Row was built later. Wooden boardwalks (later gravel paths) connected the clubhouse to many of the cabins so that the ladies would not ruin their shoes in the mud. The summer community, which populated the rustic cabins from June to Labor Day, was made up mainly of people from Knoxville. Fish and game from the mountains were available for the table, as were fine foods shipped by train from Knoxville. Ice, packed in sawdust, was brought from Maryville by train. Electricity was provided a few hours a day from an electric generator, operated first by waterpower and then by a diesel generator.

A rival resort community, Wonderland Park, was created a few years later, in 1912, in Elkmont near the Appalachian Club. In 1914, the Wonderland Park Hotel and associated buildings changed hands to become the Wonderland Club, owned by private members of an association. An annex to the hotel was built in 1920. Some of the rooms in the hotel and annex were privately owned by individual members but could be rented when the owners were not in residence.

The Little River Railroad traveled daily from Knoxville to Elkmont in a trip that took two and a half hours each way. Tradition has it that rivalry between members of the social clubs was so intense that they would barely acknowledge each other on the train.

The property owners of the Appalachian Club and Wonderland Park were able to transfer their property to the National Park with lifetime leases. Eventually the most of the leases were transferred to 20-year leases, expiring in 1971. Most of those leases were ultimately extended to 1992. The preservation of surviving portions of these of these historic communities has been an ongoing controversy.

This view shows the village of Elkmont as it looked around 1908–1909. (Great Smoky Mountains National Park Archives.)

In this photograph, a group of men is standing on the steps of the Elkmont Post Office. From left to right, these men are Lee Trentham, Dallas Owenby, Jack Young, S. W. Henry, and Doc Webb. (Great Smoky Mountains National Park Archives.)

In this photograph from around 1915, W. E. "Doc" Webb, Knoxville native and inventor of the medicine Ex-Lax, clowns for the camera, pretending to be drunk on moonshine. Doc is holding a mason jar, presumably of illegal brew. Note the wagon and the team of oxen, possibly Levi Trentham's team. (Great Smoky Mountains National Park Archives.)

Levi Trentham (1852–1936) of Elkmont did contract work for the Little River Lumber Company, both logging and grading roadbeds for the railroad. Trentham also operated a tub mill on Jake's Creek in Elkmont, as well as a small country store. Because he was illiterate, he would draw pictures of items bought on credit and keep the pictures on nails on the wall of the store until the debt was paid. Levi Trentham is buried at the small cemetery in Elkmont. (Great Smoky Mountains National Park Archives.)

In this photograph, guests are assembled on the porch of the Appalachian Club House in 1917. Note the sign posted on the wall in the left of the photograph, which loudly proclaims "Rule 8"—no dogs allowed on the porch of the clubhouse. (Thompson Collection, Calvin M. McClung Historical Collection.)

This photograph shows the original Appalachian Club House at Elkmont as it looked around 1910, when it was newly built. This structure burned in 1932 and was replaced with a smaller clubhouse. (Emma Hope, Calvin M. McClung Historical Collection.)

The "curly ash foot log" seen in this photograph provided a primitive footbridge across Jake's Creek near the Appalachian Club House at Elkmont around 1910. (Great Smoky Mountains National Park Archives.)

This interior photograph of the Appalachian Club House shows the reception/sitting room. Note the elk's head over the fireplace and the spinning wheel on the hearth, which were purely decorative features. The elk has not been known in the Great Smoky Mountains since the earliest days of European settlement. (Thompson Collection, Calvin M. McClung Historical Collection.)

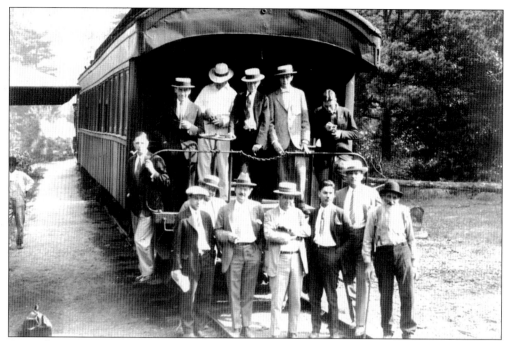

Around 1925, a group of visiting dignitaries pose for a photograph on the caboose of the train at the Elkmont depot. Year-round Elkmont resident Levi Trentham is at the far right. Russell Hanlon is next to Trentham, and Col. David Chapman is the fifth person from the right. (R. Hanlon, Calvin M. McClung Historical Collection.)

In 1913, the Little River Lumber Company deeded land to the Appalachian Club for a playground and swimming pool. The "swimming pool," shown here in July 1914, was built by damming the Little River and clearing some of the rocks from the riverbed. The water was crystal clear and ice cold. (Thompson Collection, Calvin M. McClung Historical Collection.)

The Rufus J. Hommel family is seen in this photograph sitting on the porch steps of their cottage at Elkmont in the 1920s. Note the boardwalk in front of the fence that led to the clubhouse. The boards proved to be slippery and were later replaced with gravel. Hommel created a large commercial apple orchard at Elkmont after 1917. (Thompson Collection, Calvin M. McClung Historical Collection.)

The Eppes family is seen in this photograph in front of their cottage at Elkmont in the 1920s. (Thompson Collection, Calvin M. McClung Historical Collection.)

The interior of the Schuerman cottage at Elkmont is seen in this photograph from around 1920. Some of the cottages were more substantial and more elaborately furnished than others. (Thompson Collection, Calvin M. McClung Historical Collection.)

The Little River Railroad took Girl Scouts to Camp Margaret Townsend in the 1920s because there was no road for automobiles to travel to the camp. Alternate transportation was provided by the railroad motorbus fitted to ride the rails. In this photograph, the bus is shown traveling on the tracks, possibly on its way to Tremont. (Thompson Collection, Calvin M. McClung Historical Collection.)

This photograph shows three of the brochures created by the "Knoxville & Augusta and Little River Railroads" in the early 20th century to promote visits to "the Elkmont country." Railroad timetables were included. (Great Smoky Mountains National Park Archives.)

This photograph shows "Happy Landings," the Elkmont home of Alice Townsend, widow of Col. W. B. Townsend. The home was destroyed by fire in 1968, shortly before Alice's death. (Great Smoky Mountains National Park Archives.)

The Wonderland Park Hotel was built in 1912 on land acquired from the Little River Lumber Company by Knoxvillians John P., Charles, and A. E. Carter. In 1914, the hotel was sold to a group of Knoxville investors, who renamed it the Wonderland Club. This photograph shows the Wonderland Club as it looked on September 9, 1921. (Thompson Collection, Calvin M. McClung Historical Collection.)

The Little River Railroad train arrives at the depot at Wonderland Park in July 1914. (Thompson Collection, Calvin M. McClung Historical Collection.)

This photograph shows the reception/sitting room of the Wonderland Club as it looked in 1938. (Thompson Collection, Calvin M. McClung Historical Collection.)

These ladies are seated at a table on the porch of the Wonderland Club around 1930. They do not appear entirely happy to be photographed. The original caption for the photograph simply reads, "The Gossip Club." (Thompson Collection, Calvin M. McClung Historical Collection.)

Camp Townsend for Boy Scouts was established around 1915 in Elkmont near the Wonderland Club. In 1923, the camp became a private summer camp named "Camp LeConte for Boys," which was run by John Gore, former director of the scout camp. Archery, as seen in this photograph from around 1930, was one of the skills taught at camp. (Thompson Collection, Calvin M. McClung Historical Collection.)

Camp LeConte had two buildings, 17 tent sites, and 10 acres for recreation. It operated until 1954. Shown are the parade grounds and tents around 1930. (Thompson Collection, Calvin M. McClung Historical Collection.)

A group of Girl Scouts at Camp Margaret Townsend weaves baskets in this 1927 photograph. Col. W. B. Townsend deeded 11 acres in Tremont to the Girl Scouts in 1925 and built and equipped Camp Margaret Townsend in memory of his late wife. The camp was located on the site of the cabin of Black Bill Walker, one of the most famous hunters in the mountains. The National Park Service purchased the land on which the camp was located in 1939 but granted the Girl Scouts a 20-year lease on 20 acres. The Tanasi Girl Scout Council's lease expired in 1959, and the camp closed. The site of the former camp is now the Great Smoky Mountains Institute at Tremont. (Thompson Collection, Calvin M. McClung Historical Collection.)

A group of Girl Scouts prepares food over an open fire at Camp Margaret Townsend in 1927. (Thompson Collection, Calvin M. McClung Historical Collection.)

This photograph shows the Rufus J. Hommel apple orchard at Elkmont in 1931. In 1917, the Little River Lumber Company had deeded a large parcel of land east of Jake's Creek to Rufus Hommel, who planted extensive apple orchards and built an apple barn. The barn is now a ruin. (Thompson Collection, Calvin M. McClung Historical Collection.)

In 1925, the Little River Lumber Company ceased logging in the area around Elkmont, and the Little River Railroad took up the railroad track in that vicinity. The railroad ties remained in place and were used as a roadbed for automobiles. In this photograph, Joe Myers stands next to a Ford Model T in the "road" near Elkmont. (Great Smoky Mountains National Park Archives.)

Seven

THE MOVEMENT TO CREATE THE GREAT SMOKY MOUNTAINS NATIONAL PARK

The effort to create a national park in the Great Smoky Mountains began as early as the 1890s. In 1923, Stephen Mather, the director of the newly created National Park Service, officially announced his support for the creation of additional national parks in the eastern United States. Several different potential park sites were actively promoted. The creation of a national park in the Great Smoky Mountains, despite its scenic beauty, proved to be an uphill battle.

Civic leaders in Tennessee and North Carolina responded to the challenge. Ultimately the Great Smoky Mountains Conservation Association took the lead in Tennessee in promoting a national park. The government of North Carolina appointed an 11-member statewide commission to push for the creation of a national park. In 1925, Asheville boosters of the project were incorporated as Great Smoky Mountains, Inc. The Parks Commission and the U.S. Congress ultimately designated not one potential national park but two—one in the Blue Ridge Mountains of Virginia and the other in the Great Smoky Mountains in Tennessee and North Carolina. But the money to purchase the land would have to be raised by supporters of the projects. A long and difficult period of fund-raising ensued. The tipping point was the pledge from John D. Rockefeller Jr. for a gift of up to $5 million as a memorial to his late mother, Laura Spelman Rockefeller.

Funds became available for purchasing land for the park in 1928, but the acquisition of land proved to be contentious and difficult. The Depression made funds pledged in better times difficult to collect. A number of smaller landowners who owned family farms in the Smokies bitterly resisted removal. The federal government finally had to step in and provide a major allocation to buy the balance of the land needed to make the Great Smoky Mountains National Park a reality. The date of the passage of this allocation—June 15, 1934—is now commonly accepted as the official birth date of the Great Smoky Mountains National Park. The final land acquisitions were then completed to establish the minimum boundaries needed for the park to become a reality. The Civilian Conservation Corps built much of the infrastructure for the new park during the 1930s.

A very important component of the interest groups lobbying to create the national park were members and supporters of the "good roads" movement of the 1920s. This political cartoon from the *Knoxville Journal* of May 16, 1927, advocates building an automobile road through the future park to connect Sevierville and Gatlinburg with Bryson City, North Carolina. Automobiles were correctly seen as the key to developing tourism in the Great Smoky Mountains. (R. Hanlon, Calvin M. McClung Historical Collection.)

Pres. Franklin D. Roosevelt and First Lady Eleanor Roosevelt visited Knoxville on November 17, 1934. Here he receives a Red Cross pin from Knoxvillian Jamie Hall. The presidential visit was to inspect the construction of Norris Dam by the Tennessee Valley Authority. President Roosevelt visited the Great Smoky Mountains National Park only once prior to the dedication in 1940. In June 1937, on his way to a political event in Chattanooga, President Roosevelt and his party stopped briefly to visit the park, but his visit was marred by heavy rain. The first lady visited the new park for several days in April 1937 with her secretary and took several trips from her base in Gatlinburg, exploring scenic areas of the park. (Thompson Collection, Calvin M. McClung Historical Collection.)

David Chapman is standing at the front in this photograph, to the right of the man holding the sign. Chapman and the park supporters were met by a crowd of 500 people and by the marching band of Knoxville High School at the Louisville and Nashville (L&N) Railroad Station on their return from Washington on April 30, 1931. David Chapman (for Tennessee) and E. C. Brooks (for North Carolina) just returned from successful negotiations in Washington, D.C., brokered by the National Park Service, to purchase land from the Champion Lumber Company for the Great Smoky Mountains National Park. (Thompson Collection, Calvin M. McClung Historical Collection.)

A group of hikers are seen in this photograph taking a brief rest on a hike up newly named Mount Chapman. They are Harvey Broome (left), honoree David Chapman (front), and Knoxville photographer Jim Thompson (right). These men were leaders of the Tennesseans promoting the creation of the park. Both Chapman Highway (Highway 441) and this peak in the Smokies were named for David Chapman. (Thompson Collection, Calvin M. McClung Historical Collection.)

One of the most prestigious supporters of the movement to create the Great Smoky Mountains National Park was Horace Kephart of North Carolina, the author of *Camping and Woodcraft* and *Our Southern Highlanders*. Both books have remained in print for many decades. Kephart learned about the Great Smoky Mountains and their people by living in the mountains from 1903 until his death in an automobile accident in 1931. The portrait seen here was made by his close friend George Masa, a Japanese-American photographer who lived in Asheville from 1915 until his death in 1933. Masa also worked hard to see the park created. A peak in the Great Smoky Mountains was named for Horace Kephart, and a scenic overlook was named for Masa. (Great Smoky Mountains National Park Archives.)

This group of hikers is setting up camp, probably in the mountains in North Carolina, around 1922. George Masa of Asheville, who is in the second row on the far left, is possibly serving as their guide. The hikers are most likely the friends or family of Mary Rothrock, who is on the far right in the front row. George Masa, a Japanese-American who settled in Asheville, was a talented photographer who deeply loved the Great Smoky Mountains. (Mary U. Rothrock, Calvin M. McClung Historical Collection.)

These hikers have just set up camp on Mount LeConte in July 1925. Manning McCarter, one of the oldest frequent hikers of Mount LeConte, is standing at the far left in front of the tent. (Thompson Collection, Calvin M. McClung Historical Collection.)

Jim Thompson took this carefully composed photograph of members of the Smoky Mountains Hiking Club at Myrtle Point on Mount LeConte in the 1920s. The observation tower is at the left of the photograph. (Thompson Collection, Calvin M. McClung Historical Collection.)

Jack Huff, seen in this photograph taken at LeConte Lodge in 1927, was the first caretaker/operator of the lodge on top of Mount LeConte. He has a gun in his hand and a basket-style backpack. Pictured here is the "kitchen," with an open fireplace for cooking, tables, and a cabinet for storage. (Thompson Collection, Calvin M. McClung Historical Collection.)

A group of hikers are standing at the "outdoor kitchen" at the lodge on Mount LeConte in 1927. Note the coffee pot on the barbecue pit. (Thompson Collection, Calvin M. McClung Historical Collection.)

Rainbow Falls is one of the premier waterfalls in the Great Smoky Mountains. Located on Mount LeConte about halfway up the Rocky Spur trail, the falls drop about 85 feet from a rock ledge to the basin below. This photograph, taken around 1925, shows the falls under a normal flow of water. On days like this one, hikers can walk behind the falls. (Thompson Collection, Calvin M. McClung Historical Collection.)

This photograph from the 1920s shows the Chimney Tops viewed from the cabin at Bear Pen Hollow. This view was photographed many times and was painted by Knoxville artist Charles C. Krutch in 1934, the last painting he completed prior to his death. (Thompson Collection, Calvin M. McClung Historical Collection.)

The state line and crest of the Great Smokies are seen here around 1928. This photograph was taken from the Gant Lot, one of the grassy balds in the southern part of the Great Smoky Mountains where cows and sheep were pastured in the summer months before the creation of the park. (Thompson Collection, Calvin M. McClung Historical Collection.)

This photograph shows the line separating the states of Tennessee and North Carolina along the crest of the Great Smoky Mountains near Thunderhead around 1930. (Thompson Collection, Calvin M. McClung Historical Collection.)

Two hikers stand at "Charlie's Bunion" (viewed from the west side) on the Appalachian Trail, four miles northeast of Newfound Gap. The rock outcropping is similar to other nearby peaks in the Sawtooth Section, but it is more rugged. In 1925, a fire following extensive logging left the mountain open to massive erosion during heavy rains. Eventually only bare rock remained. (Thompson Collection, Calvin M. McClung Historical Collection.)

A flock of sheep is seen here grazing on Gregory Bald, one of the grassy mountaintops above Cades Cove, around 1928. (Thompson Collection, Calvin M. McClung Historical Collection.)

The Great Smoky Mountains provide a panoramic backdrop to a view of the Sugarlands Valley in the 1920s. Today the fences are gone, and the pastures returned to forest decades ago. (Thompson Collection, Calvin M. McClung Historical Collection.)

A hiker is seen in this photograph dipping drinking water from a cold mountain stream in the 1920s. At that time, this was seen as relatively safe. Unfortunately, this is no longer the case. (Thompson Collection, Calvin M. McClung Historical Collection.)

This photograph was used by promoters of the Great Smoky Mountains National Park in the 1920s to prove the size and majesty of the virgin hardwood forests still standing in the mountains after years of heavy logging. The young man stands next to the huge tulip poplar to give a sense of scale. (Thompson Collection, Calvin M. McClung Historical Collection.)

Two fishermen enjoy trout fishing in the 1930s. Logging and erosion had depleted the population of fish. Restocking the fish was a priority of the new park from the beginning. (Thompson Collection, Calvin M. McClung Historical Collection.)

These nine hikers set off to attempt the first documented hike of the crest of the Great Smoky Mountains through the new park from August 7–15, 1932. The group traveled from White Rock to Deal's Gap. This photograph shows the nine hikers at the summit of the Smokies at Clingman's Dome, next to the mile marker (elevation 6,642.8 feet), which was placed there by the U.S. Geological Survey. The hikers, from left to right, are as follows: (first row) Carter Whittaker of Atlanta; Harvey Broome, hiking club president; Warren Hall of Atlanta, president of the Georgia Appalachian Trail Club; and Walter Berry; (second row) Charles Cornforth; Charles Gibson; Carlos Campbell; Herrick Brown of Greeneville; and Guy Frizzell. (Harvey Broome, Calvin M. McClung Historical Collection.)

The intrepid hikers are seen here setting up a campsite on their long trek. (Harvey Broome, Calvin M. McClung Historical Collection.)

Camping in the Great Smoky Mountains, even in 1932, required a permit from the park. Here park patrolman John B. Carroll (second from right) checks the permits of the nine hikers. (Harvey Broome, Calvin M. McClung Historical Collection.)

The nine hikers at the end of the 72-mile hike are standing in front of the highway construction crew's garage near Deal's Gap. With nine days growth of beard, the scruffy hikers traveled from Deal's Gap to Maryville and then by bus from Maryville to Knoxville. Carlos Campbell noted that other bus passengers gave the hikers, who sat at the back of the bus, as much distance as possible. (Harvey Broome, Calvin M. McClung Historical Collection.)

The Tallassee Lodge is shown in this photograph from around 1930. The resort was outside the southern end of the Great Smoky Mountains National Park and across the river from the Tallassee Post Office and railroad depot. (Thompson Collection, Calvin M. McClung Historical Collection.)

This interior view shows the reception/sitting room of the Tallassee Lodge around 1930. The lodge was developed by J. L. Caton and failed a few years after it began. (Thompson Collection, Calvin M. McClung Historical Collection.)

Jim Thompson took this photograph of a cabin in Boogertown in 1936. The road from Gatlinburg to Pigeon Forge at that time ran mostly on the western side of the river. This picturesque house with a wood shake roof stood near what is now the north end of the tunnel and was linked by a swinging bridge to the road. Carlos Campbell wrote an interesting account of the process of shooting the photograph. Thompson tried out five or six views in three different spots before he found just the one he wanted. This photograph was used as one of the illustrations in an article in *National Geographic* magazine in August 1936 by Leonard C. Roy titled "Rambling Around the Roof of Eastern America." A number of photographs by Thompson and Campbell were used as illustrations for this article. (Thompson Collection, Calvin M. McClung Historical Collection.)

The photograph shows one of the many mills on creeks in the Great Smoky Mountains in the 1920s. There were 13 mills on Mill Creek alone. This one appears to be a tub mill—one with its wheel turned horizontally to the running water underneath. (Thompson Collection, Calvin M. McClung Historical Collection.)

On August 7, 1931, Charlie Gibson (with the wheel) and Harvey Broome posed on Sharp Rock (White Rock), five miles from Waterville, North Carolina. The two hikers traveled 70 miles from this starting point to measure the exact distance of the Appalachian Trail, climbing the crest of the Smokies three different times. (Harvey Broome, Calvin M. McClung Historical Collection.)

From August 6 to August 18, 1931, Harvey Broome and Charlie Gibson, members of the Smoky Mountains Hiking Club, hiked and measured the Appalachian Trail from Mount Guyot to Newfound Gap. "Dutch" Roth joined the two hikers to bring additional supplies. This photograph shows their crude shelter at a camp about 200 feet below Low Gap in North Carolina. Gibson (left) and Roth are seated in the camp. The metered bicycle for measuring distance is on the right side of the photograph. (Harvey Broome, Calvin M. McClung Historical Collection.)

Members of the Smoky Mountains Hiking Club helped blaze trails through the new park, but actual trail construction was done by Civilian Conservation Corps workers. (Thompson Collection, Calvin M. McClung Historical Collection.)

Civilian Conservation Corps workers were the primary builders of the infrastructure of the new park between 1933 and 1942, when the program ceased because of the outbreak of World War II. The workers lived in temporary camps at places such as Cades Cove, Smokemont, and Sugarlands, and built trails, roads, and stone bridges. In the 1930s, T. L. Yon, foreman, instructed the enrollees on stonecutting and building with stone. Bridges like this double-arch bridge from the 1930s are a surviving testament to their craftsmanship. (Thompson Collection, Calvin M. McClung Historical Collection.)

This photograph shows the clouds and fog settled on the lower elevations of Mount LeConte in 1930. The poetic title, given by the photographer, is *Above the Clouds*. (Thompson Collection, Calvin M. McClung Historical Collection.)

This panorama of the Great Smoky Mountains was taken on October 24, 1932. It is titled simply *Barnett's Knob*, which is a peak on the border of the park and the Cherokee Reservation. (Thompson Collection, Calvin M. McClung Historical Collection.)

Eight

VANISHED COMMUNITIES OF THE GREAT SMOKY MOUNTAINS

As the idea of the Great Smoky Mountains National Park began to take shape in the 1920s and 1930s, it was not yet clear that the people of the mountains would be booted off their farms by the forced acquisition of their land for the new park. An early concept for the park had promoted the idea that the farmers who wished to do so would be allowed to remain on their land and continue farming as a "living history" exhibit for tourists. But as the park administration adopted the concept of returning most of the land to a wilderness rich in plant and animal life, the forced removal of most of the small farms became a necessity. The John Oliver family of Cades Cove pursued a legal fight all the way to the Tennessee Supreme Court against the use of eminent domain to take their land. They lost.

Mountain communities, some of which had existed for several generations, were largely dispersed, and a unique way of life vanished from the highest mountains in eastern North America. It had persisted for just over a century. By selectively removing many of the houses and farm buildings from the park, the history of the people in the Great Smoky Mountains was rewritten. Places like Greenbrier, Cades Cove, and Cataloochee have lost much of the evidence of their past. Only a few isolated examples of "pioneer" log cabins and buildings are left to tell the complex story of these families and communities that lasted for three or four generations. Most of the communities that existed when the park was created are now gone. Only chimneys, sometimes fallen, and lingering flowers, like spring daffodils, hint at the vanished past.

This early photograph shows a vista of Cades Cove. The floor of the cove, ringed by mountains, is now encircled by a loop road 11 miles long. The cove has a larger cluster of surviving "pioneer" homesteads than any other part of the park and is one of the most popular automobile destinations there. (Harvey Broome, Calvin M. McClung Historical Collection.)

Pictured from left to right, Sam Sparks, Hubert Cable, Fonz Cable and John Cable rest by the fence at the Cable Mill in Cades Cove on May 4, 1936. John Cable (standing) was 81 years old at the time. (C. S. Grossman, Great Smoky Mountains National Park Archives.)

Tom and Jerry Hearon hew a new main shaft for the Cable Mill in Cades Cove during repairs to the mill in December 1935. (C. S. Grossman, Great Smoky Mountains National Park Archives.)

Sherman Myers is "snaking" a log down a hillside in Cades Cove with a team of horses. (Randolph Shields, Great Smoky Mountains National Park Archives.)

Rhodie Abbott was the sister of Kate Lawson of Cades Cove. She is shown here in a pensive moment around 1930. (Exline, Great Smoky Mountains National Park Archives.)

Dan Myers was a lifelong resident of Cades Cove. At age 83, in March 1937, he sits in front of a fence on the site of his birthplace on North Cove Road. Myers told Carlos Campbell that he made his first trip to Spence Field at age 16 in 1869 and that the "field" was then largely a forest of beech trees, not the grassy pasture known later. (C. S. Grossman, Great Smoky Mountains National Park Archives.)

Tom Hearon is shown hewing and riving (splitting) log shakes for the Kate Lawson house in Cades Cove in November 1936. (C. S. Grossman, Great Smoky Mountains National Park Archives.)

This photograph shows a baptism in Cades Cove around 1915. A group of well-dressed spectators watches the proceedings from the bank. (Randolph Shields, Great Smoky Mountains National Park Archives.)

The building pictured here around 1935 served as both the church and the schoolhouse for the Little Greenbrier community of the Great Smoky Mountains. (Thompson Collection, Calvin M. McClung Historical Collection.)

Four pupils gather in the doorway of the Little Greenbrier School in March 1936. The school closed permanently with the end of that term. (Exline, Great Smoky Mountains National Park Archives.)

The Walker sisters were perhaps the most famous residents of the Great Smoky Mountains National Park from the 1930s to the 1950s. Of the seven Walker sisters, only one—Caroline—married. John N. (called Hairy John for his long beard) and Margaret June Walker had 11 children in all. The boys married and moved away from the homestead, but the six remaining daughters lived out their lives in the family home. The first to die, Nancy, passed away in 1931; Louisa, the last of these sisters to die, passed away in 1964. This photograph shows all seven Walker sisters around 1909. Pictured, from left to right, they are as follows: (first row) Margaret, Louisa, and Mary Elizabeth (Polly); (second row) Hettie, Martha, Nancy, and Caroline. (Great Smoky Mountains National Park Archives.)

The front view of the Walker homestead in Little Greenbrier, pictured here around 1930. The porch was an outside workspace in warm weather. The Walker family reluctantly sold their farm to the park in 1940 with a life estate for the five remaining sisters. Until 1953, the sisters encouraged visitors to the park to visit with them as they worked. Old age and illness forced the hospitable sisters to curtail visits by tourists after that year. (Thompson Collection, Calvin M. McClung Historical Collection.)

The family of George H. Caldwell of Cataloochee poses in front of their house in 1902. Each member of the family, with the exception of the eldest daughter, is wearing a piece of clothing made by the mother all the way from the "sheep's back" to finished clothing. Before George Caldwell died in 1928, he advised the family "not to have a lawsuit with the Park but to sell their home for what they could get for it." (Great Smoky Mountains National Park Archives.)

May Caldwell, the widow of George H. Caldwell, poses by the chimney of their home in Cataloochee. In 1937, at the time of this photograph, she was 80 years old. She donated to the park her loom and spinning equipment, which she used to make handmade cloth from 1880 to 1912. The brick in the chimney was pressed by hand in groups of four and burned in a nearby kiln on the grounds of the house. (H. C. Wilburn, Great Smoky Mountains National Park Archives.)

The miller of the Mingus Mill on the North Carolina side of the Park is shown in a rare interior view of the mill in action around 1935. (Great Smoky Mountains National Park Archives.)

A group gathers on a bridge on the banks of the Oconoluftee River at Smokemont to watch a baptism around 1920. (Exline, Great Smoky Mountains National Park Archives.)

This large group of hikers stands above and below Abrams Falls in the mid-1920s. The basin at the foot of the falls, which is near Cades Cove, is one of the deepest in the park. (Thompson Collection, Calvin M. McClung Historical Collection.)

Adam Carver, age 91, is seen crossing a foot log on Braden Fork in November 1937. Carver was one of the builders of the Mingus Creek Mill. His comment on trying to cross the foot log at his age was straightforward: "It is point blank aggravating. I can't walk a log like I used to." (H. C. Wilburn, Great Smoky Mountains National Park Archives.)

Nine

GATLINBURG

The gateway for many visitors from Tennessee into the Great Smoky Mountains National Park has long been the village of Gatlinburg. Established in the first years of the 19th century, Gatlinburg was originally known as White Oak Flats. The name was changed to Gatlinburg in 1860, when a post office was established in the store of a new arrival, Radford Gatlin. Gatlin was soon driven from the community, allegedly because of his views in favor of slavery and secession from the Union, which most mountain people did not share. In the early years of the Civil War, Gatlinburg was occupied by troops from Thomas's Legion of Cherokee soldiers from Qualla, who were put there by the Confederate army to protect supplies of saltpeter, used for making gunpowder, mined at Alum Cave Bluff on Mount LeConte. A small contingent of Union troops drove the Confederates out of Gatlinburg in 1863. The short battle has been described as the last battle between Native Americans and whites in the eastern United States. Gatlinburg remained small and isolated through the rest of the 19th century, with very poor roads connecting it to the outside world. In the 1890s, the trip by wagon from Knoxville to Gatlinburg took a minimum of 18 hours.

In 1910, the Pi Beta Phi fraternity of college women decided to establish a settlement school in Gatlinburg. At that time, Gatlinburg consisted of only six houses, three general stores, and one church, but there were some 200 families in the surrounding mountains and valleys who wanted their children to have a greater educational opportunity than was afforded by the one-room school typical of the time. The teachers at the school played a pivotal role in helping revive traditional mountain crafts. The sale of handicrafts provided additional income for mountain families. The fraternity marketed items nationally through its network of alumnae clubs and locally in Gatlinburg in the Arrow Craft Shop. With the coming of the Great Smoky Mountains National Park in the 1930s, the village of Gatlinburg grew into a resort town, catering to the large numbers of tourists drawn to the park. Hotels, tourist courts, service stations for automobiles, restaurants, and gift shops sprang up to meet the needs of tourists along the two main roads that converge to form the heart of Gatlinburg.

This view, taken around 1925, shows the town of Gatlinburg, nestled under Mount LeConte. (Thompson Collection, Calvin M. McClung Historical Collection.)

A horse, drawing a sled, is hitched in front of a country store in the vicinity of Gatlinburg around 1920. (Harvey Broome, Calvin M. McClung Historical Collection.)

This photograph, taken by Harvey Broome around 1920, shows a farm in the vicinity of Roaring Fork above Gatlinburg. Note the cultivated field of corn rising on the steep hillside behind the cabin. (Harvey Broome, Calvin M. McClung Historical Collection.)

The Gatlinburg Baptist Church is seen here in the 1920s. (Harvey Broome, Calvin M. McClung Historical Collection.)

The Mountain View Hotel started by A. J. "Andy" Huff of Gatlinburg is seen here around 1925. An addition had been made in front of the original building by this time. (Thompson Collection, Calvin M. McClung Historical Collection.)

The new Mountain View Hotel in Gatlinburg is seen here in the 1940s, complete with people on horseback ready to ride mountain trails and an open touring car for the use of guests. (Thompson Collection, Calvin M. McClung Historical Collection.)

The reception/sitting room of the new Mountain View Hotel is seen in this photograph from around 1940. Note the display of photographs of the Great Smoky Mountains and the handwritten sign for sightseeing tours to the left. The rocking chairs and the distant fireplace look enticing. (Thompson Collection, Calvin M. McClung Historical Collection.)

A typical room in the Mountain View Hotel is seen in this photograph from around 1940. The room is paneled in wood. Much of the furniture was locally made in Gatlinburg. (Thompson Collection, Calvin M. McClung Historical Collection.)

A view from a distance showing the Mountain View Hotel in its mountain setting is seen in this photograph from around 1940. The same view today would be virtually unrecognizable except for the mountains in the distance. (Thompson Collection, Calvin M. McClung Historical Collection.)

Lydia Whaley is standing in front of her home in Gatlinburg. She was one of the foremost authorities on local history and lore. (Great Smoky Mountains National Park Archives.)

Russell Hanlon Sr. operated the Quaint Shoppe and Great Smoky Mountains Museum in the 1930s in Gatlinburg. This photograph of the store from 1931 shows the exterior of the building. The "museum" was a collection of artifacts of mountain life. The shop specialized in mountain handicrafts. (Thompson Collection, Calvin M. McClung Historical Collection.)

Russell Hanlon Sr. built one of the first outdoor amusements for tourists in Gatlinburg. This miniature golf course was built in front of his cabin in the 1930s. Here some young people are seen playing the course, which was lit by electric lights strung overhead. (R. Hanlon, Calvin M. McClung Historical Collection.)

Hattie Maples Ogle (later McGiffin) (1898–2002) is seen in this photograph, taken in the 1930s, standing in front of the handicrafts store she started in Gatlinburg. Her father Isaac "Squire" Maples operated a store in Gatlinburg, where she became expert in evaluating furs brought in by hunters. In 1939, she started the Bear Skin Tourist Court. She continued to take an active part in family business enterprises until near the end of her life. (R. Hanlon, Calvin M. McClung Historical Collection.)

Tom Ogle, son of Hattie and Charles Ogle, walks toward his bicycle in this Gatlinburg street scene from the 1930s. He is standing beside the parkway, looking towards the park. On the left side of the street was Isabelle Lumas's French Tavern, an early Gatlinburg restaurant. (R. Hanlon, Calvin M. McClung Historical Collection.)

THE ARTIST SHOP

CLIFF DWELLERS
GATLINBURG TENN

The Cliff Dwellers shop in Gatlinburg was built in the 1930s by Louis E. Jones and was operated by him and his wife until 1955. Jones sold his paintings and etchings of the Great Smoky Mountains, as well as fine arts and crafts. The Cliff Dwellers had an unusual Swiss-chalet look, which made it a downtown landmark until 1995, when the Cliff Dwellers was threatened with demolition. Artist Jim Gray and his son Chris moved the historical building to property adjoining their Church Mouse Gallery on Glades Road outside Gatlinburg, where it stands today. (Calvin M. McClung Historical Collection.)

Louis and Emma Jones are seen together in this photograph, taken in the 1940s. Jones moved from Woodstock, New York, in 1928 and settled permanently in Gatlinburg in 1933. He was one of the first year-round resident artists of the Great Smoky Mountains. (Calvin M. McClung Historical Collection.)

113

This photograph, taken in June 1937, shows the workshop of Mack McCarter in Gatlinburg. Clyde Huskey and Mack McCarter are seen here making straight-back chairs on the porch of the shop. Note the "Houses to Rent" sign on the porch. (Alan Rinehart, Great Smoky Mountains National Park Archives.)

Pictured here in 1938, Joe Williams (left) and Timothy Quilliams (right) attend the annual "Old-Timers Day" held in Gatlinburg. (Great Smoky Mountains National Park Archives.)

A group of stylishly dressed women are seen in this photograph bringing their hand-woven coverlets to the Pi Beta Phi Fair in Gatlinburg on "Old-Timers Day" in 1936. (Great Smoky Mountains National Park Archives.)

Ernest and Lucinda Ogle and their daughters Frances and Billie pose on a tractor in this photograph. The family was selected to be the representative East Tennessee family and was given a trip to the New York World's Fair in 1939. (Great Smoky Mountains National Park Archives.)

This photograph from 1938 shows the then-new Riverside Hotel in Gatlinburg. Guests on horseback are ready to ride out on mountain trails nearby. (Thompson Collection, Calvin M. McClung Historical Collection.)

The craft revival movement, started in Gatlinburg by the Pi Beta Phi Settlement School in 1912, continued to grow and prosper in the subsequent decades. The Arrow Craft Store in Gatlinburg has been a longtime venue for the sale of local handicrafts, especially textiles, pottery, and woodcarving. This photograph shows the store around 1940. (Thompson Collection, Calvin M. McClung Historical Collection.)

Ten

THE DEDICATION OF THE PARK AND THE YEARS AFTER

Even though June 15, 1934, is celebrated as the date of the creation of the Great Smoky Mountains National Park, the park was not officially dedicated until six years later, in 1940, on the eve of World War II. The funds to acquire the remaining land needed for the park were appropriated by Congress in 1934, but the process of acquiring the land took a number of years. The Civilian Conservation Corps began building the park's trails, roads, and bridges in the 1930s, but much still remained to be done when Pres. Franklin D. Roosevelt officially dedicated the Great Smoky Mountains National Park on Labor Day, September 2, 1940. The entrance of the United States into World War II just over a year later slowed the development of the park.

The park began to draw larger numbers of tourists in the postwar years. The growth of Gatlinburg continued, but tourism began to affect other areas as well. Pigeon Forge had long been a small farm community along the Little Pigeon River, between Gatlinburg and Sevierville. In 1930, the population of Pigeon Forge was estimated at 200. Residents were mostly farmers who tended the lush fields of corn, wheat, peas, and hay that flourished in the rich river-bottom soil. In 1961, a generation later, Pigeon Forge was incorporated and tourism had begun to transform the village. The level expanse of Highway 441 had been converted into a four-lane, divided highway in the early 1950s. The number of hotels had grown to 75 by 1965. In 1961, the Roberts brothers, who operated the Tweetsie Railroad in the mountains north of the Park, created a new type of attraction in Pigeon Forge, the Rebel Railroad. In 1970, the Rebel Railroad changed hands and became Goldrush Junction. In 1977, Jack and Pete Herschend bought Goldrush Junction and converted it into Silver Dollar City, a theme park based on their original park, created in Branson, Missouri, in 1960. The Herschend brothers became partners with Dolly Parton in 1986, when Silver Dollar City was transformed into Dollywood. Now doubled in size and drawing over two million visitors a year, Dollywood is Tennessee's most visited tourist attraction, aside from the Great Smoky Mountains National Park itself.

Pres. Franklin D. Roosevelt dedicated the Great Smoky Mountains National Park on Labor Day, September 2, 1940. First Lady Eleanor Roosevelt and a host of dignitaries were included in the party. The dedication took place at the Laura Spelman Rockefeller Memorial at Newfound Gap. This photograph shows the speakers and honorees assembled on the stone terrace above the crowd. (Thompson Collection, Calvin M. McClung Historical Collection.)

Pres. Franklin D. Roosevelt is seen making the keynote address at the dedication of the park. He smiles for the camera of *Knoxville Journal* photographer Jimmy Myers. (Myers Album, Calvin M. McClung Historical Collection.)

This photograph shows the new parking lot for automobiles at Newfound Gap in the 1940s. The short hike up to Clingman's Dome has traditionally been one of the most popular stops for park tourists. (Thompson Collection, Calvin M. McClung Historical Collection.)

Bus service from Knoxville to Gatlinburg began as early as the late 1920s. The last stretch of the road from Sevierville to Gatlinburg was paved in 1925. This photograph, taken in 1936 for Reeder Chevrolet, shows riders of the "Smoky Mountain Transit Co., Inc." bus with hats or pith helmets and walking sticks, ready to brave a trip to the mountains. (Thompson Collection, Calvin M. McClung Historical Collection.)

Tourists began to visit the park in even larger numbers in the 1950s. Advertising photographs, such as this one, were used in brochures and publications to encourage tourism. These stylish young women from the late 1940s are reading the plaque commemorating the life of Cherokee leader Tsali. (Thompson Collection, Calvin M. McClung Historical Collection.)

Gatlinburg entrepreneurs began to promote Gatlinburg as a place to ski during the winter. Here a stylishly dressed young woman holds a pair of skis in a carefully posed photograph taken on a snowy mountain in the late 1940s. (Thompson Collection, Calvin M. McClung Historical Collection.)

Horseback riding on trails near Gatlinburg was a popular pastime for tourists in the 1940s. Here a group of riders prepares to set out from the Mountain View Hotel. (Thompson Collection, Calvin M. McClung Historical Collection.)

The "sky lift" began operation in Gatlinburg in 1954. A quick trip up Crockett Mountain provided a panoramic view of the city and the mountains. This was the first sky or ski lift in the southern United States. (Thompson Collection, Calvin M. McClung Historical Collection.)

As black bears became acclimated to large numbers of tourists in automobiles, the bears became less fearful. (Paul M Fink, Calvin M. McClung Historical Collection.)

Although the park rangers emphatically warned against feeding black bears, tourists were often tempted to do so, oblivious to its danger. This photograph from the 1950s shows someone taking a foolish risk. (Paul M Fink, Calvin M. McClung Historical Collection.)

By the 1950s, the Ole Smoky Mountain Candy Kitchen was already established in Gatlinburg. It is still famous for its salt-water taffy. (Thompson Collection, Calvin M. McClung Historical Collection.)

R. L. Maples built the Hunter Hills Theater, an outdoor amphitheater, outside Gatlinburg in 1956. It first featured the historical drama *Chucky Jack: The Story of Tennessee*, based on the life of John Sevier and written by Kermit Hunter. In the opening season in 1957, young Knoxville actor John Cullum played the role of Sevier. The University of Tennessee theater program later operated the theater, performing such plays as *Dark of the Moon* for tourists in the summer season. (Thompson Collection, Calvin M. McClung Historical Collection.)

The Old Mill on the Little Pigeon River in Pigeon Forge is the most historic surviving structure in the thriving tourist town. At the time of this photograph around 1940, tourist development had barely begun. (Thompson Collection, Calvin M. McClung Historical Collection.)

Hill-Billy Village in Pigeon Forge is packed with shoppers in this photograph from the 1950s. Still a popular stop for souvenirs and postcards, the village is one of Pigeon Forge's oldest businesses. (Thompson Collection, Calvin M. McClung Historical Collection.)

Another major tourist attraction in Pigeon Forge in the 1950s was the Fort Weare Game Park, which featured snakes, other reptiles, and some exotic animals. Note the farmland behind the Game Park and motel. (Thompson Collection, Calvin M. McClung Historical Collection.)

The "Smoky Poky," a miniature train, offered rides for children in Pigeon Forge in the 1950s. (Thompson Collection, Calvin M. McClung Historical Collection.)

One of the more interesting and educational tourist attractions in Pigeon Forge was the Pigeon Forge Pottery, established in 1946 by Douglas Ferguson and Ernest G. Wilson, who had worked together at TVA's Ceramic Research Laboratory in Norris in the 1930s. The pottery used local clay to make a variety of figurines, bowls, pots, and other pieces. This photograph shows the pottery in 1956 and a sign inviting tourists to "see it made." (Thompson Collection, Calvin M. McClung Historical Collection.)

A group of employees of the Pigeon Forge Pottery are seen in this photograph from the 1950s applying glazes of special clays, which changed color as the pieces were fired in the kiln. (Thompson Collection, Calvin M. McClung Historical Collection.)

Knoxvillian Harvey Broome (left), a founder of the Wilderness Society, which was a precursor of the Sierra Club, is seen in this photograph taken in 1962 with John Parris (center) and Supreme Court Justice William O. Douglas (right). Douglas was an avid outdoorsman and wrote an enthusiastic and well-illustrated article on Cades Cove, which was published in *National Geographic* magazine in 1962. Parris, a storyteller from Asheville, is getting a laugh from both of his traveling companions. (Harvey Broome, Calvin M. McClung Historical Collection.)

Wiley Oakley (1885–1954) was widely known as "the roamin' man of the Mountains," a phrase he invented to describe himself. He was truly a larger-than-life figure from the years before and after the Great Smoky Mountains National Park was created. A great storyteller, his homespun humor caused him to be compared to Will Rogers. In his early years, Wiley became well known as a guide for hunters and fishermen. Later he guided hikers and tourists who visited the new park. His intimate knowledge of the geography of the mountains and the native plant and animal life made him an invaluable resource for park personnel. Wiley Oakley lived all of his life in the vicinity of Gatlinburg, in the shadow of the mountains he loved. He is buried in the White Oak Flats Cemetery in Gatlinburg. (Louis E. Jones postcard, Calvin M. McClung Historical Collection.)

ACROSS AMERICA, PEOPLE ARE DISCOVERING SOMETHING WONDERFUL. THEIR HERITAGE.

Arcadia Publishing is the leading local history publisher in the United States. With more than 3,000 titles in print and hundreds of new titles released every year, Arcadia has extensive specialized experience chronicling the history of communities and celebrating America's hidden stories, bringing to life the people, places, and events from the past. To discover the history of other communities across the nation, please visit:

www.arcadiapublishing.com

Customized search tools allow you to find regional history books about the town where you grew up, the cities where your friends and family live, the town where your parents met, or even that retirement spot you've been dreaming about.